How to Survive a DUI Arrest:

What You NEED to Know

2nd Edition

By Michael Chastaine
Attorney at Law

Additional copies are available at special quantity discounts for bulk purchases, to be used for sales promotions, premiums, fundraising, and educational use.

For more information, please contact:
support@chastainelaw.net (916-932-7150)

Contact the author directly at: **mike@chastainelaw.net**

Learn How the Chastaine Law Office has Helped Others Get Optimum Results after Their DUI Arrest:

THE ONLY LAWYERS FOR ME

"The Chastaine Law Office is the only law firm I will go to for any of my legal needs. They represented me in a recent case and achieved everything I was hoping to accomplish. Their knowledge of the law, dedication, and hard work made it possible to resolve issues I wished to leave in the past. From start to finish, they kept me informed concerning the progress of my case."

–Criminal Defense Client, Sacramento, CA

"Michael, as a lawyer, seems to have an uncanny knack for cutting to the chase. As an investigator, he is one of the easiest attorneys to work with or for. He understands, as a professional, that you know your job. He gives you the freedom to be creative and do that job. This equates to clients getting the most from their legal defense team."

–Rodney O. Harmon, *Private Investigator, Harmon Investigations*

"Michael is the consummate professional -- articulate, informed, ethical, consistent, committed, and with great integrity!"

–Lori R., Sacramento, CA

"Over the years, we have used several different lawyers, due to distinctive needs we had. There is no question that Michael Chastaine is at the top of the list in his field. He did an excellent job winning our case. There was never a time when he was not available to take a call – even

giving us his cell phone number. When faced with a criminal charge, having your lawyer available and communicative with you is probably the single most important reassurance you can have. He is the finest in his profession, and we will be eternally grateful for his outstanding work."

–Mary O., Sacramento, CA

I appreciate Mr. Chastaine's candor and professionalism. He was honest, open and thorough when explaining the steps necessary in order to reach the goals that I had set forth. Because of his expertise, I was able to reduce my felony conviction and probation. I cannot thank him enough and his staff enough.

-Danielle N., Sacramento, CA

<u>Acknowledgements</u>

This is the second edition of this book.

I want to thank Amie Beighley who co-authored the first edition, for her help and advice.

My thanks to Elisa for her continued support, love and encouragement.

My thanks also to all the people who have supported my efforts to provide outstanding legal representation to our community.

Table of Contents

Introduction

By Michael Chastaine,

Founder of the Chastaine Law Office

Bill called me one day. He had been arrested for a DUI. He was scared, nervous and did not know where to turn. He came in to the office and discussed his situation in a safe and confidential setting. Bill asked lots of questions. I answered all I could, but some I simply did not have enough information to be able give an opinion as to the final outcome. When we completed that first meeting, Bill was still concerned but now he knew that he was not alone. By retaining me, he had an attorney that cared about him and what would happen. He could sleep at night.

I got right to work. I was able to prevent the automatic suspension of his driver's license. I subpoenaed important records such as the in car camera so I could see what the police saw. I discussed with Bill what was going on in his life and made recommendations that were specific to his personal situation. We worked together and developed strategies that made sense. As I did the research to find answers, I made sure that Bill stayed informed. In the end, armed with a full and complete understanding of the facts I was able to make a presentation to the prosecution that convinced her that the charges should be reduced to a wet reckless. After Bill completed probation, I successfully petitioned the Court to dismiss the case.

While not every case ends in a reduction of charges, this is my process. I take the time to listen to my clients and actually hear what they have to say. I do my best to answer all of the questions that I can and find out the answers to those questions that require a closer look. I work with my clients to develop strategies that will work, and I negotiate with the prosecution to obtain the best outcome available. If necessary, I take the case to a jury and fight to the very end.

This is why I am successful. Knowledge is power. Experience has no substitute. But listening to my clients is the most important thing that I can do to obtain the best outcomes. I know what questions to ask and I give my clients the time and respect to work through the process.

No one expects to be arrested for driving under the influence (DUI). For most people, when it happens, it is a real eye-opener and likely a SHOCK. Your neighbors, co-workers, and the community at large, see these charges as very serious, because of the thousands of lives lost each year in accidents that involve drivers who were under the influence. Even more people are impacted in life-changing ways because of injuries sustained in accidents. The ripple effect of these incidents widens the circle to an even broader scope that includes spouses, children, other family members, and employers. So many lives are potentially affected when a person makes the decision to get behind the wheel after having too much to drink. Among the lives impacted is yours. The pain and shock of finding yourself in this predicament can become overwhelming and difficult to manage.

What makes driving under the influence different from most other crimes is that there is rarely any intention to break the law. Simply put, DUI is a crime of poor judgment. The driver is "influenced" to falsely believe that his or her ability to drive a vehicle is sound. Most offenders truly believed they were OK to drive. Once the damage is done, it is common to hear the driver say that they didn't have much to drink and, had they known their blood alcohol level was so high, they never would have driven. If the driver had known all of the consequences, they would have called a cab or a friend to pick them up. But now, unfortunately, he or she has to deal with the severe and often tragic consequences.

It is easy to become very "down on yourself" if you have been arrested for a DUI. Being charged with DUI has nothing to do with who you are, as a person. This is one crime that anyone who consumes alcohol, or other substances, is capable of committing. DUI does not discriminate. People of all races, ethnicities, gender, age, and socioeconomic status are charged with DUI. Every case is as unique as the person being charged. In order to gain the very best outcome possible, hiring a trained professional attorney is vital. Without proper legal training and experience, you by yourself have no way of knowing how to approach the situation to assure you receive the very best outcome. The professionals at a criminal DUI law firm, such as mine, know exactly how to approach your case.

I have written this book to give you important information at a time when your level of confusion and fear is possibly at the highest point it will ever be in your adult life. I want to give you a clear idea of the process that you can expect to encounter, as well as the different variables that could impact your case. I practice law exclusively in Northern California, concentrating on clients mostly in Sacramento and the surrounding counties. As you read this, remember that the laws to which I refer are specific to these regions. Laws do change from place to place, but the general information is applicable in most states.

It is my hope that you will never need this information. If you are already in this situation, I want to let you know that this is not "the end". You WILL get through this. On the other side of the charges, you will likely emerge with a new outlook— having become wiser from the experience and able to make better decisions involving alcohol and driving.

I am hopeful that young people, in particular those who may have just received their driver's licenses, will gain insight from these pages. If you are reading this book today—for yourself or a loved one—consider sharing it. **It could just save a life.**

Why Did I Get Busted?

This scenario may be all too familiar to you: Driving home, after having a few drinks with friends, you notice flashing lights in your rearview mirror. For a moment, you hope the officer is after someone else, but it soon becomes clear that he wants you to pull over. You know you had a couple of drinks, but you're pretty sure you're "OK". What did you have – a couple of beers, a few glasses of wine, or maybe some mixed drinks, over a couple of hours? Well wait... Maybe you did have a shot or two, and maybe it was more than just a couple of drinks!

You pull over and provide your driver's license, registration, and insurance information. You are asked to step out of the car and perform a series of field sobriety tests. Sure you are nervous, but you think you did pretty well. Then, the officer asks you to blow into a preliminary alcohol screening devise (PAS). The next thing you know, they order you to turn around and place handcuffs on your wrists. At that moment, hundreds of thoughts flash through your mind. You are put into the back seat of the police car and are driven to a holding facility – either the county jail or a police station. When the department deems that you are sober, you are released with a court date in hand.

Now what?

The first thing you may be asking yourself is, "Why did I get arrested? I wasn't hurting anyone; I was just trying to get home."

The fact is you got busted because the officer believed that you were driving under the influence. Why did they think that? It could have been because of the manner in which you were driving. It could have resulted from the fact that you were just leaving a bar at two o'clock in the morning. It could have been that there was a mechanical issue with the car and, when they approached the car, they smelled alcohol on you. For whatever reason, the officer ran you through a series of tests, including the PAS test. Based upon the results of those tests and the officers' training and experience, they formed the opinion that you were driving under the influence. Right or wrong, it's yours to deal with now. You have to navigate the Department of Motor Vehicles (DMV) if you want to keep your license. And that is only the beginning. Next you have to deal with the court system. You may have to address an inquiry by a professional licensing board. If you were involved in an accident, a lawsuit may also be another complicated set of obstacles to handle.

One of the main reasons that people get DUIs is that they believed one of the many popular "drinking myths". First, when the PAS is administered, many people are stunned by the alcohol level they register. Many people believe that there was no way they drank enough to register an alcohol level that is above the legal limit, i.e. .08% BAC (blood alcohol concentration). It's very common for me to hear clients say, "I had only one drink an hour."

Here is how the Department of Motor Vehicles identifies "one drink".[1]

- One 12-ounce beer with an alcohol content of approximately 5%-6%
- One four-ounce glass of wine
- 1.5 ounces of 80% hard alcohol

The problem is usually this: bars and restaurants serve drinks in larger quantities than the amount that the DMV model counts as "one drink". For example, most people consider a pint of beer to be one drink. Yet 16 ounces is four ounces larger than the DMV's 12-ounce beer allotment. Those extra four ounces can add up quickly.

Another potential pitfall could be the amount of alcohol in your favorite beer. Today, many popular craft beers contain an alcohol content that can be as high as 10% ABV (alcohol by volume), as compared to the 5%-6% found in the DMV model. In considering drink equivalents, it's not just the ounces one has to worry about.

It is also extremely common to be served "a double" when ordering a single shot of liquor. When

---

[1] When you renew your driver's license, the DMV will send you a chart that contains these guides to blood alcohol levels.

we do the math, every shot could contain up to three ounces of alcohol – meaning that, for every shot, you have actually consumed TWO drink equivalents rather than the ONE per hour. Another issue is that, when ordering mixed drinks that contain multiple types of alcohol (such as a Long Island Ice Tea), drinking one such drink is more like drinking two-and-a-half to FIVE drinks!

The last variable involves the bartender. DMV calculations are based upon measuring and pouring exact amounts. If the bartender is "freehand pouring", the amount of alcohol is usually higher. With all of these scenarios, it is possible that just one drink could put you over the legal limit.

For those who are wine connoisseurs, it is typical for one pour to be six ounces, or more, at a restaurant or wine bar. Unless you request a four ounce pour, you could be consuming one-and-a-half drinks instead of the one you thought you ordered. Wines on the average are steadily increasing in alcohol content"...*a "typical" table wine might have been between 11% and 12% alcohol 10 years ago, it may be at least two or even three percentage points higher today."* (Wall Street Journal, April 23, 2010; Wines that Pack a Little Extra Kick)

Bottom line is this: many people think they are controlling their alcohol intake, keeping it within the guidelines, while dining or enjoying drinks with friends, when in fact they are consuming well above the DMV limits.

Why is Driving Under the Influence so Dangerous?

Alcohol is a depressant. It causes a person's central nervous system to slow down. This slowing impairs "psychomotor", or reaction skills, and "cognitive", or thought-processing skills. These impairments distract from the business at hand—driving. These are proven facts. Even blood alcohol levels as low as .02% (well below the legal limit) can impact an individual's capacity to reason and focus.[2]

According to the National Highway Traffic Safety Administration, an estimated 10,322 people died in drunken driving crashes in 2012. This is 31% of all traffic deaths that year.[3] And 1,174 of those deaths involved persons under the age of 21. This is more than three young people dying each day.

Motor vehicle crashes are the leading cause of death for 15 to 20-year-olds in the United States. Among 15 to 20-year-old drivers killed in a fatal accident, 32% of these drivers had been drinking and 26% had a blood alcohol level of .08 or above. [4]

---

[2]http://www.duifoundation.org/drunkdriving/impairment/operating/

[3] www.responsibility.org

[4] National Highway Traffic Safety Administration Traffic Safety Facts "Young Drivers," 2013

Every two minutes, a person is injured in an accident involving a drinking driver. The cost of drinking and driving is $199 billion a year.[5]

Consider these impacts:

- Costs derived from drunken driving are not just limited to those directly involved in the accident. The lives of entire families, friends, and co-workers are impacted by the death or injury of persons involved in DUI-related crashes. Financial, emotional, and psychological damages are only the beginning of what they experience.
- Loss of income and work hours can have a grave impact on employers and businesses.
- First responders – police, firefighters, ambulance drivers, medical personnel who experience the carnage that can occur after an accident involving a driver under the influence – are affected.
- Each day, every county courthouse in California will have at least one department filled with people accused of driving under the influence. The cost to the criminal justice system is enormous.

---

[5] National Highway Traffic Safety Administration. "The Economic and Societal Impact of Motor Vehicle Crashes, 2010. "National Traffic Safety Administration, 2014, DOT HS 812 013. http://www-nrd.nhtsa.dot.gov/Pubs/812013.pdf

The costs -- in both lives and money, caused by drinking and driving -- can be catastrophic. It is not difficult to understand, both legally and morally, why driving under the influence is illegal. The people involved in the justice system – the police, judges, district attorneys, and probation officers – all know the facts. If you understand that these officials have witnessed many DUI situations, you will begin to understand why the system works the way it does.

Attitude with the Police

In 2010, for my 50th birthday, I travelled to Queensland Australia to compete in a 10 day expedition race called XPD. The total race distance was over 450 miles of mountain biking, trekking and paddling. After about three days we were trekking through the Outback. We had 60 kilometers (about 36 miles) of barren, scrubby hills to navigate through to locate the next transition point. Hour after hour we trekked on. For almost the entire distance, there was not a manmade object or road anywhere to be found. It felt like we would never finish. Traveling day and night I only had my compass, my map, my teammates and my attitude. By working together, as a team, maintaining a good attitude and good old perseverance, we managed to find our way. It took us over 40 hours. In the end we finished 13th out of 40 teams in this international field. Over half the teams dropped out.

On these long events, the single most important tool I possess is my good attitude. Having a bad attitude drags down the entire team, sucks away valuable energy and simply gets in the way of success

As with most things in life, controlling and maintaining a good attitude will be very important throughout the process. The better you are able to do this, the greater your chance of gaining a more favorable outcome. The importance of having a good attitude starts at the side of the road, when dealing with the police officer. It is also very important when working with your attorney, when you appear in court, and throughout every step of the process.

When the arresting officer is communicating with you, your approach will be crucial in setting the stage for how you are treated. Being cooperative is very important. If your PAS and field sobriety tests are border line, a respectful attitude could mean the difference between the officer giving you the benefit of the doubt and allowing you to go, or choosing to arrest you. Even if the officer opts to follow through with the arrest, a cooperative attitude will improve your chances of a more favorable police report. It will certainly improve the way you are treated. If you are cooperating and are respectful, the interaction with the cop will be better, and you may even be able to convince the officer not to tow your car.

Remember, the officer that you interact with has likely seen the aftermath of many injury-related accidents involving drunken drivers. Each time a police officer performs a car stop, their life hangs in the balance, as it is among the most dangerous actions they must perform. When an officer approaches a car, he or she never knows what they will encounter. Risks are high, especially in the dark of night and when the incident is in the path of other vehicles on the road. You can make the encounter safer for everyone involved by following basic directions -- staying in the car, not moving suddenly or suspiciously, and following the officer's instructions.

Even though the officer may arrest you, it is the district attorney who will ultimately determine what charges to file. The district attorney will review the police report and the chemical tests and will decide whether to file charges. If the police report reflects that the officer found you to be cooperative, that you followed directions, you did OK on your field sobriety tests (even if you did not fully pass), the district attorney may determine that these are all indications that you were not under the influence. If the Blood Alcohol Content (BAC) is equal to, or just above the legal limit, the district attorney knows that a good attorney can contest the results and that the prosecutor may have a tough time proving the case against you. I have had a number of cases where my client was arrested, but the district attorney did not file charges. In every single one of those cases, my client maintained a good attitude and was extremely cooperative with the police officer. The importance of this cannot be overstated.

On the other hand, for those who have a bad attitude with the police officer, it is certain that this will be noted in the report. Being uncooperative, belligerent or rude are all elements that will be used as evidence that you were drunk. To be certain, the police officer will not cut you any breaks, and if you are too uncooperative, you could receive further charges of resisting arrest or even assault on a police officer. When the district attorney reads this type of report, you can expect to have every possible charge filed against you, and the court may tack additional time on to your sentence. **Don't be that guy.**

Attitude with Your Attorney

If you are wondering whether or not you need an attorney, the simple answer is "Yes". (I address this in the chapter, **Why You Need an Attorney,** later in this book.) When you hire or are assigned an attorney—regardless of whether they are a private attorney or a public defender---your attitude interacting with them is very important.

Your lawyer is part of your team. Blaming your attorney for your situation is not productive; in fact, it's just the opposite. Your attorney is your greatest ally, and your strongest asset in gaining the very best results from a difficult situation. It is vital that you trust your attorney and agree to follow the advice your attorney provides for you.

How to get the most from your legal counsel:

First, be honest with your attorney. Everything that you tell them is confidential. It will not be repeated without your consent. You must share everything you can remember about what really happened. You can expect a good attorney to ask questions like these:

- What is going on in your life?

- Are you going through any other legal troubles?
- Are you in the middle of a divorce, did you just lose your job, or are you experiencing any other type of crisis?
- Has drinking become a problem in your life?

In order to best assist you, your attorney needs to know what is going on in your life.

Second, follow your legal counsel's advice. If your lawyer tells you to attend AA meetings, for example, you need to do so. Your attorney is not suggesting such measures to inconvenience you. When your attorney provides this type of advice, they are doing so to strengthen your position with the court and to improve the outcome of your case. I am not saying that you should blindly do whatever you are told. Remember that you are a team, and if you disagree or don't understand the advice you are given, then you need to speak up immediately and get clarification. Take the time to understand why the advice is being given. If, after having a full discussion about the merits of the advice, you still disagree, you may want to consider obtaining new counsel. Think carefully about your decision, however. Throughout this kind of crisis, you must consider who has the experience and expertise in this area. It is important to remember that your attorney has been down this road before. Your attorney does have your best interest in mind. **The two of you are a team.**

Attitude with the Court

Just as respectful, cooperative behavior is important when interacting with the police officer and your attorney, the same is absolutely necessary when you are in the courthouse and standing before the judge. Behaving like a jerk before the judge is *never* a good approach. It is also important to be respectful to all of the court staff, including the clerks and bailiffs. If you mistreat them, it will get back to the judge. Just remember that, from the moment you walk into the courthouse, everyone is watching. You need to be on your best behavior.

I am often asked: "What should I wear when I go to court?" Think of your court appearance as if you are going to a job interview. You are hoping to make a good impression, so dress appropriately. For men, a suit never hurts. Wearing a tie is not required, but is a nice touch. It demonstrates that you care about what is happening, and you are showing respect for the judge. For women, dressing in business attire is also a good idea. Do not wear clothing that you would wear on a date. Instead, wear something you would consider wearing to church. Again, you will be sending a message that says, "I care about what happens here, I know you will be making a decision that affects my future, and I take this very seriously."

Arrest and Bail

When you are arrested, one of three (3) things will happen:

- You will be released with a court date and promise to appear.
- You will have to post bail in order to be released.
- You will remain in jail until at least your first court appearance.

In most California counties, you will be released "on a promise to appear" on a first time DUI offense without an accident. This is also known as "OR" or "Own Recognizance". When an OR is ordered, you sign a document that says you promise to appear in court at the designated date, location and time. Your attorney can appear on your behalf. If that date arrives and neither you nor your attorney appears, the court will issue a bench warrant for your arrest.

Other California counties require a person to post bail before being released in even the simplest first-time DUI cases.[6] Posting bail simply means that you are giving the court money or a lien on property, as your assurance that you will appear in court. Bail is normally determined by the county's

---

[6] El Dorado County requires bail in every case.

bail schedule and, in most counties, it is posted online.[7]

There are three ways to post bail.

1. Cash or a credit card is taken to the jail and is posted.
2. A property bond is posted.
3. A bail bondsman is engaged to post a bond with the court on your behalf, for a fee.

If the cash or credit card option is selected and the bail is $10,000, you give the court $10K to hold. When your case is completed and you have made all of your court appearances, you will get your money back. Most people do not choose this option because their money is then tied up for the duration of the case. The advantage of this method is that all of your money is returned to you, or is applied toward your fines, should the court levy fines as a result of your charges.

When a property bond is selected, you must post a lien against any real estate that you own. When bail is very high, a property bond is often the only way to accomplish obtaining your release. To be eligible, you must have twice the equity in the property as the amount of bail. For example, if your bail is set at $10,000, you need a current appraisal

---

[7] In Placer County in 2015, bail for a first time DUI was $5,000. If there is a BAC over .15 it is $10,000. In Sacramento County in 2015, a DUI with injury – bail is $50,000. The amount of bail varies county to county.

showing at least $20,000 in equity. Another downside to this option is the requirement of obtaining a current appraisal—a process that can cost several hundred dollars and take a week or longer.

The most common way to post bail is to use a bail bondsperson. In this scenario, you contract with a bail bondsperson, who posts a bond with the court, for a fee. In most cases, the fee is 10% of the bail. If bail is $10,000, for instance, your fee will be $1000. Your bondsperson's fee is not refundable. Fees are typically lower for those who have engaged an attorney—usually a 2% reduction.

In some cases, a person is not released from jail. There could be several reasons for this:

- If you are from out of town or do not have a stable home, the court might determine that there is a high risk that you will not return for your court date.
- If you have a serious criminal history, you might be held in jail until you can post bail.
- If there is an accident and someone is injured or killed, a very high bail may be issued and you may have to post the entire amount of the bail before you are released.

If you are not released from jail, the law requires you be brought before the court within 72 hours. This first court appearance is called an arraignment. During this appearance, you will be formally advised of the charges filed against you, and you can request that the court review and adjust your bail. At this time, the court could release you, reduce bail, or possibly even increase bail.

Hiring an attorney to *immediately* begin working on your case is *very* important, particularly if you have not been released from jail. If you choose a public defender, none will be appointed until your first court appearance. This means you will be in custody for (at the very least) a couple of days before you have an opportunity to speak to your appointed counsel.

When you hire a knowledgeable attorney, there are many things he or she can address for you, before your first court appearance. The first, and likely the most urgent action, is to address the issue of bail and to get you out of custody. Knowing your options and making the necessary financial arrangements could make the difference between sitting in jail and being released. Sometimes, the only real option is for you to be released into an alcohol treatment program. These are individual assessments that require a meaningful consultation with YOUR skilled and knowledgeable lawyer. The sooner this is done, the more options you will have.

The DMV and your Driver's License

Our lives have become dependent on driving. We rely on this privilege for going to work, to the store, and for carrying out our everyday functions. However, driving is NOT a right; it is a privilege -- one that can be taken away.

The Department of Motor Vehicles (DMV) and the criminal courts work separately. The DMV determines whether or not your driver's license is suspended or revoked.[8] It is possible for the DMV to suspend your driver's license, even when the district attorney does not file any charges. It is also possible to avoid a license suspension, even though you are convicted of a drinking driver-related offense. The important point to understand here is that the DMV operates on its own and may make independent determinations, regardless of what the district attorney or court does.

In your dealings with the DMV, time is of the essence. If you have a Blood Alcohol Concentration (BAC) of .08% or above, you have ten days from the date of your arrest to request a hearing. Once a

---

[8] There are certain convictions that require a mandatory suspension. There is also a mandatory license suspension, if you refuse to take a chemical test. However, most of the time, the DMV and the court run on separate tracks.

hearing is requested, your driver's license remains valid until the hearing is held and a determination is made. If you fail to request a hearing, your license will be automatically suspended. This is a hard-and-fast rule, and it doesn't matter if you are in the hospital or injured in a crash. You OR your attorney may file this request.

Another important factor to note is this: If you are released from jail, your court date will NOT be within the DMV's ten-day window. If you choose to use a public defender, remember that he or she will not be appointed until after the ten-day period. Thus, you will not have the benefit of legal assistance during this critical period. (See chapter: **Why You Need an Attorney**.)

Once a hearing with the DMV has been requested, a number of important things can be done. First, you can now obtain the police report much faster than you can get it from the district attorney. (I know it sounds surprising that the DMW would be more efficient then the district attorney, but it is true!) Second, you can subpoena important documents and records. And thirdly, if your license is going to be suspended, you can exercise some control over when the license suspension would go into effect.

Getting the police report before your first court appearance gives you, "the defense", the advantage of obtaining the records that your lawyer will want to review. Your lawyer can then study important aspects of your case, such as the in-car camera footage from the police stop, and the calibration records for the PAS and breath-test machines. It also allows for any other investigation to take place right away. Learning the facts and seeing the evidence, sooner rather than later, can make all of the difference for your defense.

The DMV hearing is pretty informal and is conducted by an administrative hearing officer. This person is not a judge, or even a lawyer, but rather is an employee of the Department of Motor Vehicles. This is not to say that they have no legal training, but such training IS limited.

The DMV cares about only two things: First, were you legally detained? There is a lot of variation regarding when the police can legally pull your car over (or even if your car was actually pulled over). There are hundreds of cases that deal with this Fourth Amendment issue. When you have an attorney who understands this area of law, you have a definite advantage.

The second thing the DMV cares about is whether your BAC (blood alcohol content) was .08 or higher. (The California DMV does not deal with drug DUI's.) The determination as to whether your BAC was .08 or higher, will be based upon the tests done during your arrest process.[9] However, since the

---

[9] Refusals to be tested are an entirely different situation and

test did not occur when you were actually driving, the result may or may not accurately reflect your BAC at the time you were driving. BAC levels rise and fall, and your BAC, while you were driving, may be higher or lower than the test result taken at the station. Also, the method in which the sample was taken, how it was stored, and the type of test used to measure the BAC can impact the final result.

The ability to contest the BAC level is the province of forensic labs and forensic experts. While a good lawyer can help greatly, he or she cannot refute the test result without an expert. Your attorney's engaging of the best experts and facilities to challenge the test result may be the only opportunity to prevent a conviction. Even in the administrative hearing at the DMV, a solid expert that is fortified with the correct records may be the only chance of saving a person's license, when the BAC was measured by law enforcement at over .08.

A DMV hearing can be done in person or by phone, including any testimony by an expert or by any witness. How such a hearing is conducted will be determined by your attorney, based upon the evidence. While my office has successfully defended driver's licenses against the DMV process, most DMV hearings contesting a BAC of .08 or higher will not succeed. The only chance one has for success is for the case to be properly investigated by someone with experience, like the experts just described.

---

normally cause an automatic suspension.

Your DMV findings will not be revealed on the same day as the hearing. A written order will be sent to you (and your attorney) by mail, usually within a week or two. If you lose the hearing, you have the right to request a department review of the decision, as well as the right to appeal the decision to the County Superior Court. These requests must be made within a certain time period, depending upon the laws affecting your case. You will be required to pay a fee. Your attorney will be able to counsel you on the merits and costs of following this course of action.

Criminal Proceedings

You have a right to be present at every court appearance. However, you may waive this right and direct your attorney to appear on your behalf.[10] When you hire a private attorney, in most circumstances, your lawyer can make all of the court appearances without you. If you are representing yourself, or are being represented by the public defender, you will be required to appear in court.

The court is required to give you "due process", and in order to be found guilty, the prosecution must prove your guilt "beyond a reasonable doubt" to the satisfaction of twelve independent jurors. (See Chapter on **Jury Trial**.) Due Process requires that you be given notice of the crime for which you are charged and be provided with "discovery" (copies of the police report, lab reports, statements that you made and any other documentation that law enforcement obtained.)

You have a right to a public and speedy trial. You can waive this right, and most clients do. If you remain in custody, you have a right to be brought to trial within 30 days. If not in custody, you have a right to be brought to trial within 45 days of the date of your arraignment.[11] The decision as to whether to

---

[10] In California, this is pursuant to Penal Code Section 977.

proceed in a "time not waived" posture is a strategic determination to be made by you and your attorney. Normally, time is waived to give your attorney the time needed to obtain and review all the necessary records. Some of the records, such as the testing device logs, have to be obtained by subpoena, and this process can take time. If an expert is required, arranging for them to appear, according to their schedule, can prevent one from going forward under a "time not waived" position.

The district attorney (on behalf of the State of California) also has a right to a speedy trial. This means that you cannot drag your case out forever. Eventually, the court will insist that you either resolve your case or set it for jury trial. How much time the court allows the matter to be continued depends on many factors. However, it is rare for the court to allow a case to be continued for more than six months before setting it for jury trial.

Finally, you have a right to cross-examine any witness brought against you. You have the right to present a defense and to use the court's subpoena power to compel witnesses to come to court. You have the right to testify on your own behalf, if you choose. You also have an absolute right to not testify or to make any statements.

---

[11] California Penal Code Section 1382.

Court Appearances

There are different types of court appearances. Many times, several of these various appearances are combined. It is possible to be arraigned, to have a pre-trial conference, to enter a guilty or no-contest plea, and to be sentenced, all in one appearance. Sometimes these appearances are separated out to different dates. The How and Why depends upon your goals and legal strategy.

Possible court appearances:

- Arraignment: This is your first appearance. The court will provide you (or your attorney) with a written document, called a "complaint". It will advise you of the actual charges being brought against you.
- Pre-trial Conference: This is where your attorney can conference with the district attorney (and possibly the judge) to attempt to negotiate a settlement in your case.
- Motions: In some cases, your attorney may file motions and/or subpoenas for records. Potential motions include a motion for discovery, a motion to suppress evidence, a motion to dismiss, and/or a motion for the return of subpoenaed records. Not every case will have motions. These various types of

motions are all case-specific and may not be applicable in your case.

- Sentencing. Usually, the same day that you enter a "no contest plea",[12] if you decide to do so.

In state courts, many of these appearances will appear to be very informal. You (or your attorney) may actually address the court for only a minute or two. The entire court room may look like a three-ring circus, with attorneys scurrying around, while negotiating and trying to resolve cases. Things can happen fast. If you don't know what is going on, be sure to discuss it with you attorney, so that you understand what is happening and how it might impact you.

---

[12] In California courts, one normally enters a "no contest" plea rather than a guilty plea. This has the same effect in the criminal court. However, a "no contest" plea to a misdemeanor charge cannot be used against you in any related civil case, such as an accident.

Jury Trial

If your case cannot be resolved through an agreement, then a jury trial is set. This is the most formal of court proceedings, and it entails many rules and procedures. Here, you are the one on trial, and everyone is watching you to see how you will react. Dressing and acting properly is very important. Your attorney should thoroughly prepare you for this event. If your attorney does not set up time to prepare you, you should ask about how to dress, how to behave, and what you can expect to experience.

The first thing that will occur are Motions in Limine. These are basically the ground rules for the trial. Decisions will be made regarding what evidence will be admitted and what, if any, will be excluded. In a "standard" DUI case (one where it is a factual dispute, rather than a legal dispute); the motions may be limited and basic. If there is a dispute regarding the actual law that applies, this hearing can be more significant. Jury instructions may be discussed and decided during this phase, as well.

After the Motions in Limine, jury selection will occur. Members of the community are brought into the court room, questioned and selected by the parties. Each party (prosecution and defense) will be able to exclude potential jurors who the court agrees cannot be fair. For example, if a potential juror had a child killed by a drunk driver, they would likely be deemed to be unable to be fair in a DUI case.

Once jurors are "passed for cause" (are deemed that they can be fair), each side can exclude jurors for any reason except race, religion, sexual orientation etc. For example, if you are African-American and the prosecution attempts to exclude all African Americans from the jury, they would have to establish that they have an independent justification for the exclusion of each potential juror.

In the end, twelve jurors and one or two alternates will be selected to hear the case. These people will determine the facts, apply the law, and determine if the prosecution has proven, beyond a reasonable doubt, that you are guilty. If they do not all agree that you are guilty beyond a reasonable doubt, you cannot be found guilty. In order to reach a verdict, all twelve have to agree with either guilty or not guilty. If all twelve do not agree, then it is a hung jury, and a mistrial is declared.

If a mistrial is declared, the prosecution can determine if they want to retry the case or not. Several factors will go into making that decision, including the nature of the cause for the hung jury. For example, if ten jurors vote for not guilty and only two for guilty, it is unlikely that the prosecution would retry the case. On the other hand, if ten voted for guilty and two for not guilty, then the prosecutors may be more likely to retry the case.

Once the jury is selected, the prosecution will give an opening statement, telling the jury what it believes it can prove. The defense may also, but does not have to, give an opening statement.

Following the opening statement(s), the prosecution will present its evidence. Your attorney will be able to cross-examine each witness.

After the prosecution has put on its case, it is your turn to present your case. You may or may not testify, depending upon your legal strategy. If you choose not to testify, the jury cannot legally use your silence against you. The determination as to whether you will or will not testify is one of the bigger decisions for the defense (you and your attorney). Whether you testify or not changes the entire approach, as well as the jury's determination. In my opinion, if you do not testify, the jury focuses on whether or not the prosecution has proven its case beyond a reasonable doubt. If you do testify, the jury's focus changes to whether or not they believe you. This is a decision that can only be made in a case-by-case determination, requiring the solid legal advice of your counsel.

If you testify, it is important that you tell your lawyer what you are going to say on the stand. During one of my first DUI trials, my client told me that the car was weaving because of mechanical problems. I built the entire defense around that premise, including telling the jury in my opening statement that my client's car had mechanical issues. Imagine my surprise when my client insisted, while testifying before the jury, that there was nothing wrong with the car. We lost that trial.

After the defense presents its case, the prosecution can then present rebuttal evidence. After all of the evidence has been given, both sides give closing arguments, after which the jury is instructed by the court as to the law.[13]

After hearing all of the evidence, and receiving its instructions, the jury retires to the jury room to attempt to reach a verdict. How long this process will take depends on many factors. I have seen verdicts reached in fifteen minutes, but I have also had juries deliberate for weeks. Typically, a jury will be out for several hours.

---

[13] Some courts pre-instruct the jury before closing arguments. Either way is legal.

DUI Defenses

The prosecution must prove, beyond a reasonable doubt, that you were either under the influence of drugs or alcohol at the time you were driving, or that you had a blood alcohol content of .08% at the time you were driving. There are really only two defenses. Either you were not driving or you were not impaired (your BAC was under .08%). "I was not the driver" defense is pretty straightforward. If you were behind the wheel when the car was pulled over, the evidence is clear that you were the driver. However, in instances where the car was not pulled over right away – like in a hit-and-run accident – proving that a specific person was the driver may be more difficult for the prosecution. Obviously, if you can prove that another person was driving, that is the best defense.

The defense option of whether you were impaired, or over the legal limit, at the time you were driving hinges upon the chemical tests. The first thing for the defense to do is to determine if there are any flaws in the testing process. It is possible that the blood was drawn incorrectly or the testing was otherwise flawed. The only way to determine this is to obtain the proper records that document the apparatus. The law has requirements for the testing and calibration of these devices.

In situations where there is no blood or breath test, or if the test results are close to .08%, the question is whether you were impaired, or over the limit, at the time you were driving. This often involves a battle of the experts. Having a highly qualified expert, who can analyze the field sobriety tests, your driving history, and other relevant factors, greatly increases your chances of obtaining a favorable result.

To be clear, the factual defenses to a DUI are limited. Over the years, the law has been streamlined to eliminate many of the "technicality" defenses. However, rising-blood-alcohol defenses, meaning your BAC was higher at the time of the testing than it was when you were driving, are still available and need to be considered when the BAC is close to .08%.

Even though there may not be an absolute factual defense to a DUI in a particular case, the threat of a defense may be enough to persuade the prosecution to reduce or even dismiss a case. A proper investigation that raises viable defenses will often result in a better resolution. Without presenting at least the threat of some kind of defense, the prosecution has no motivation to make a better offer.

Legal Justifications for the Police to Stop You

The question of WHY you are stopped is important for two reasons. First, the DMV affirmatively requires that the police establish a legal justification for pulling over your car. Second, if the police do not have legal justification for pulling over your car, the evidence might be suppressed. The evidence that can be suppressed will include the police officer's observations, such as your field sobriety tests, any chemical test results, and anything that you reportedly said.

Police officers cannot lawfully pull over your car and detain you without probable cause. "Probable cause" is defined as an articulable suspicion that a crime was committed. Any traffic violation will do.[14] A non-functioning tail light, bald tires, excessive speed, weaving, or rolling through a stop sign are just a few examples of behavior that will serve as justification for an officer pulling you over. A police officer can also detain you if you are involved in an accident, parked illegally, or sleeping in your car.

---

[14] DUI checkpoints are an exception to this rule. The US Supreme Court has determined that the state has a compelling interest in eradicating drunk driving and so allows for random sobriety checkpoints in most states.

The law changes often. Recently, the United States Supreme Court ruled that, if a police officer reasonably believes that you violated the law and his mistake is objectively reasonable, the evidence will not be suppressed. The law involving these Fourth Amendment issues requires a full understanding of the facts and the law. Every case is unique and should be evaluated by a well-qualified lawyer.

Recently I litigated a motion to exclude evidence based on the fact that the police officer's version of the facts was not consistent with the video tape my client took with his IPhone. The officer said my client was drunk but the video clearly showed that this was not the case. The Court relied on the video and dismissed the case.

Successful motions to suppress evidence are rare. However, sometimes the threat of an arguable motion may result in a better outcome. A proper evaluation is critical to determining the best available defense.

Penalties

Penalties are determined on a case-by-case basis. The actual penalties in any specific case are dependent on a variety of factors: Was an accident involved? Was anyone injured? Were children in the car? What was the BAC level? The nature of the driving may influence the penalty, such as the determination of whether actual dangerous driving was involved or whether you were pulled over for a tail-light infraction. Other important factors include any prior DUI or "wet and reckless" offenses you were charged with in the last ten years.

The vehicle codes set out minimum penalties for first, second, and third offenses. However, each county has its own "standard" penalties. Some counties are much harsher than others in the application of those penalties.

Below is the range of penalties required by the vehicle code:

- First offense – Three to five years of probation, with at least 48 hours up to 6 months in jail.[15] Fine of at least $390 and up to $1000.[16] Driver's license suspension for at

---

[15] Often, the time you spend in jail when you are arrested will be sufficient for your "in jail" time. The rest can be performed through some sort of county work project – usually picking up trash in a park, or some other weekend type of work.

least four months -- although, if you sign up for the drinking driver program (which will be required), you will have your license suspended for 30 days and restricted for six months. Depending upon the county, you may have to install an ignition interlock device (IID) in your car. You may also be required to attend a Mothers Against Drunk Driving (MADD) class.

- Second offense[17] - Three to five years of probation. Ten days to one year of jail (most can be done on some kind of work program). Fine of at least $390 and up to $1000. Driver's license suspension up to two years, drinking driver program and IID installed.
- Third offense – Three to five years of probation. 120 days to 1 year in jail. Often, for a third offense, you will be required to do most, if not all, of this time actually in custody. Fine of at least $390 and up to $1000, three-year license suspension, drinking driver program and IID installed.
- Fourth offense within ten years, or injury accident -- Either of these cases turns the offense into a felony, with the potential of

---

[16] Fine: While the vehicle code mandates a minimum fine of $390, with all of the penalty assessments and associated fees that are assessed in every case, the fine will be closer to the $2,500 range.

[17] This is within ten years from the date of arrest for a prior conviction, not the conviction dates.

being sent to state prison for 16 months or more. Make no mistake that in these situations, if convicted, you will be going to jail, and your privilege to drive will be taken from you for a significant period of time.

Sacramento County. As an example, a first offense with no aggravating factors, in the County of Sacramento, will result in a person serving a minimum of 48 hours in county jail, or alternative work project. If there are other factors, such as excessive speed, a high blood alcohol concentration, accidents or driving while your license is suspended, you will likely receive increased jail time, restitution, and a lengthy DUI school. The fines and penalty assessments can, and usually do, total over $2,500.[18]

In July of 2010, Sacramento became one of four pilot counties in California to require all drivers that are convicted of a first DUI offense to install an ignition interlock device for five months.[19] This device is installed in your vehicle, at your expense. To start the car, you must blow into the device and again at random times while you are driving to monitor any alcohol intake. As of the writing of this book, there is legislation pending to have all counties in California have the same requirement.

---

[18] These local penalties are current as of January 28, 2015, and do change over time.
[19] Other counties include Alameda, Tulare and Los Angeles.

A conviction for a second or third DUI comes with more severe penalties in Sacramento County. Jail time includes a minimum of ten days in county jail or an alternative work project –four of those days must be served as continuous confinement within the county jail. Recently, the county jail stopped allowing weekend-only custody. A person must now serve the four days in a row -- which can be difficult for most, considering their jobs and other responsibilities.

The DUI School for a second DUI conviction increases to an 18-month alcohol education course which can cost as much as $1,700, and the driver's license suspension will increase to two years. One is usually eligible after 90 days to get a restricted driver's license. However, if a person was still on probation at the time he or she received a second DUI, they are not eligible for this restricted license.

A third DUI in Sacramento County has severe consequences. Though the minimum jail time is 120 days, we rarely see this offered, even without aggravating factors. The base fine and penalty assessments increase so that one can expect a total that exceeds $2,700. The alcohol education course ordered for these offenders is a minimum of 18-months, but can be extended to a 36-month course. A person can expect very serious action to be taken on his or her driver's license. There will be a three-year revocation, as well as receipt of the designation, "Habitual Traffic Offender" for up to ten years.

Placer County--a county just east of Sacramento, with its principal towns being Roseville and Auburn--is notorious for harsh DUI conviction penalties. Here, minimum offers are rare, even without such factors as excessive speed, high blood alcohol levels, or reckless driving. The minimum amount of jail time a person can expect will likely start at nine days, far above the 48 hours required by California law. Keep in mind that this is only if the blood alcohol concentration is .14% or lower. If your level is between .15%-.19%, the time will increase to between 10 and 19 days, and for an alcohol level of .20%, it will be 20+ days.

If you are charged in Placer County, you can expect very serious penalties for second and third DUIs. A person charged with a second DUI can expect to serve time in the county jail, as well as receive alternative sentencing. I have seen the offers on a second DUI begin at 60 days, without aggravating factors. To make matters worse, Placer County also has a policy requiring a person to serve at least half of that time in continuous custody, with the other half to be served on work projects or some other alternative sentence.

An ignition interlock device is not required on a first DUI conviction in Placer County. If you are convicted a second time, you are required to install one in your vehicle for a year, and the probation shifts to formal probation for four years.

The minimum penalties for a third DUI in Placer County starts with at least 180 days and increases to 364.[20] They will require all the time to be served in county jail, unless your probation officer authorizes an alcohol rehabilitation program.

Needless to say, these are significant penalties. Your only chance of having these penalties reduced is by having a strong, and experienced, attorney working with you and representing your best interests.

---

[20] In 2015, new laws passed that make the maximum time in jail for a misdemeanor 364 days, rather than the previous 365 days.

Accidents and Restitution

If you are responsible for an accident that causes damage to property or injury to someone, the court is required by law to order restitution. "Restitution" is a court order in which you pay the victim of the accident for the damage you caused -- any damage to their car or other property, and possibly their medical expenses and lost wages. The court cannot order you to pay money for what is commonly referred to as "pain and suffering".

California law provides that victims of crime are entitled to recover the full amount for any reasonable loss or expense. The prosecutor cannot agree to reduce this amount during a plea bargain, because he or she has no right to waive any claims on the victim's behalf.

The victim is entitled to collect the full amount of restitution from you, *even if the victim is separately reimbursed by an insurance payment.* However, if it is your insurance company that pays the victim, you are entitled to have the insurance payment deducted from your remaining restitution obligation.

You have the right to contest the restitution. At the time of sentencing, if the victim doesn't know the exact amount of their losses, or you wish to contest the requested amount, the court will conduct a restitution hearing.

While the "victim" has the burden of establishing the amount of damages, the district attorney represents the victim and his or her interests. The district attorney must establish that you were actually the cause of the accident. Being under the influence of alcohol does not automatically mean that you caused the accident. For example, if you were stopped at a stop light and were rear-ended, being drunk does not mean you caused the accident. The victim has the burden of proving that the defendant's criminal conduct substantially caused the victim's losses. The defendant's conduct doesn't have to be the only factor that contributed to the loss, as long as the conduct was at least a substantial factor.

Second, the district attorney must establish the actual monetary amount of the damages by presenting evidence of the amount of the actual loss. Medical bills, auto repair bills, and other records are used to arrive at a specific amount. The court may also accept testimony from the victim or other witnesses regarding the amount of the loss.

If the full amount still has not been determined at the time of your sentencing, the judge can include a provision that victim compensation will be ordered, based on an amount "to be determined" later. Even if the victim restitution amount is set at a restitution hearing, the amount can be amended, as appropriate, if the victim discovers additional losses.

If, by the end of the probation term, you have not paid all of the victim restitution, the court will convert the remaining amount into a civil judgment.

Drivers Under 21

There are different rules for drivers under the age of 21. Because it is illegal to drink in California until you are 21, it is illegal to drive with a BAC of .01% or higher. The penalties are similar to adult DUI offenses: First offense: probation, 48 hours to six months of jail, fine and license suspension for 30 days to ten months. Second offense: probation, ten days to one year of jail, fines and two-year license suspension.

There are other offenses that may come into play, such as distributing alcohol to other minors, minor in possession of alcohol, soliciting alcohol, and child endangerment. The courts and the DMV take this very seriously and will strive to send a message to the underage drinker. There are significant consequences of being charged with under-aged DUI. The ability to obtain insurance will be impacted, and current and future employers may frown upon these offenses.

Marijuana DUIs

In the state of California, it is legal to consume marijuana for medical reasons. To participate, one must obtain a recommendation to participate in the medical marijuana program established by Proposition 215. I have encountered many people who assume that because they are consuming marijuana legally, they cannot be charged with a drug DUI. However, just like with any prescription medication, you can't legally drive if such consumption has impaired your ability to do so safely.

Driving under the influence of marijuana is still considered driving under the influence of drugs. Currently it is difficult to prove someone is under the influence of marijuana. Blood tests cannot reveal when one consumed it and whether or not the particular level in one's system has an impairing effect. The National Highway Traffic Safety Administration states, "It is inadvisable to try to predict effects based on blood THC concentrations alone, and currently impossible to predict specific effects based on THC-COOH concentrations."

The government will fight an uphill battle when it comes to stating, with any amount of certainty that a person is under the influence of marijuana by simply looking at the numbers. Because there is no "magic number," a specialized officer is engaged to perform what is called a Drug Recognition Evaluation.

The penalties for driving under the influence of marijuana or other drugs are usually the same as alcohol. The specific circumstances surrounding your case -- such as whether it's your first DUI or whether you have a prior criminal history-- all play a role in how your case might resolve.

The only silver lining to a marijuana DUI is that the DMV has no power to suspend or revoke your driver's license. This does not mean your driver's license won't be suspended through the court. If that occurs, it will happen upon conviction. The main difference will be that, in a marijuana DUI case, you will not have a "hard suspension" for the first 30 days of the total suspension of six months.

Again, marijuana DUIs can be difficult to prove, based upon the fact that there is no "magic number" that indicates impairment. The prosecution has the burden of proving that you were, in fact, impaired by marijuana while you were driving.

Why You Need an Attorney

You need an attorney if you have been arrested for a DUI. Period.

Years ago, I decided that I was going to tile my bathroom. I had never tiled anything before, but I thought, "How hard can it be?" So I went to the hardware store and got a how-to book about tiling a bathroom. I spent a lot of money on the various supplies and tools needed. It took me the entire weekend and lots of sweat to complete it. While the tile in the first bathroom looked "ok", it was far from perfect. It was not so bad that I thought about tearing it out, but it was not something I was very proud of either. The second bathroom was a bit better, but still was quite amateurish-looking. In the end, if I had hired a professional to tile my bathrooms, it would have been done perfectly and looked a lot better, and I would not have used an entire weekend of my time. In the end, it would have cost less, because I would have saved the money invested in tools that I will never use again.

If you are not a trained legal professional, you simply cannot do the job as well as the person with experience and knowledge. A DUI charge is far too important to your life and your future to attempt to handle by yourself.

Do not go through this alone. The consequences are serious. There are many, many aspects of your life that will be impacted, and there are multiple ways in which you can screw this up for yourself. The results will be far more damaging and ugly than an amateur-looking tiled bathroom!

You need legal counsel.

There are basically three options regarding your legal counsel in DUI cases:

- The public defender
- Criminal law attorneys
- A criminal law attorney with a specific focus on DUI

The public defender is a licensed attorney employed by the county. Not everyone qualifies for the services of the public defender. The public defender is provided for those without the financial means to retain their own counsel. The determination as to who qualifies is made by the courts. Some are very strict and others are more liberal in appointing the public defender to those who request one. As a general rule, if you have a full-time job, you will not qualify for the assistance of the public defender.

An attorney who works for the public defender's office will typically have a lot of experience with DUIs. They are generally free or are offered at a nominal fee, as assessed by the court.

They understand the issues, can provide you with accurate legal advice, and are very familiar with the courthouse and judges. The obstacle is that a typical public defender is handling hundreds of cases at a time, and is normally unable to spend the extra time with you to determine what is going on in your life. Their workload allows only limited time to assure that you understand all of your obligations, should you ultimately plead guilty to a DUI. They will not assist you with the DMV, nor will they be able to assist you with any civil matter that might arise in the event that you are sued as the result of an accident. You will be on your own with any administrative hearings that might be related to a professional license. For example, if you are a teacher, the California Commission on Teaching Credentials might take action against your teaching credentials.

In short, a public defender's representation is no-frills. Even though the penalties may be the same, individualized attention will be limited. You will have to appear in court yourself, as it is very rare for a public defender to appear in court on your behalf. Naturally, if you really cannot afford to a hire private counsel, you certainly should choose the public defender, rather than representing yourself.

One of the big differences between a privately-retained attorney and the public defender is that the privately-retained attorney can appear in court without you present. When you work with a private attorney, you will visit the law office once and fill out your paperwork. You can (in appropriate circumstances) forego taking time off from work to attend court or the DMV hearing. This advantage will save you from taking time off from work and losing income. In many cases, the cost of hiring an attorney can be less expensive than your lost income from the court appearances. Another savings is this: your ego is spared, since most people who are arrested for a DUI feel humiliated by the experience. If you do not have to leave work for court appearances, it's very possible your employer need never know.

General criminal law attorneys will handle DUI's, but usually don't have a specific focus on that area of law. It's common to see business attorneys or bankruptcy attorneys advertising for DUI cases, since any lawyer with a bar card can appear in court on a DUI case. The court does not require any specialized training. Such lawyers may take DUI cases, because they think that it is "easy money", yet those same attorneys often have no idea what they are doing in a DUI case. It's unlikely that you will be offered the full suite of services that could be of great value in defending your DUI arrest.

If you have a driver's license, the DMV is going to be involved. While general criminal law attorneys may be very good attorneys, it is a very real possibility that they won't necessarily understand the nuances that can make a difference in the outcome of a DUI case. Because these attorneys can tend to be the least expensive, they may well provide a "barebones" representation. If they are charging only a few hundred dollars, you can expect that they will spend little or no time with you. They won't know what the important questions are, and they will merely "process" your case without providing individualized attention. It would be like taking your very expensive foreign car to the local gas station to have a motor overhaul—not a good idea. Just as with my bathroom tile experience, it will not necessarily be cheaper AND the outcome is likely to be less than optimal.

An attorney with a specific focus on DUI is the attorney or law firm that has the experience in handling DUI cases.

These professionals understand:

- How to obtain and attack chemical tests.
- How the DMV works.
- Who the best experts are.
- What the court wants to see from a client.
- How to protect your professional career.
- How to help in a meaningful way.

While these attorneys may be more expensive, you get what you pay for: a full suite of services that will allow you to rest assured that everything that *can* be done *will* be done. The few dollars more that it takes to hire the best attorney, one with an actual focus on DUI cases, is money well spent when your future is at stake.

I believe hiring a <u>local</u> attorney is important. There are firms that advertise nationally. They have big budgets and are able to buy up ads on the internet and TV. They create ways to appear that they are locally-based, but when you look at the firms' real website, you may find that they are in another part of the state or country. These firms attract business and then contract with a local attorney to make the court appearance. It's possible you may never meet the attorney who is actually handling your case. What's more, these firms are *not* inexpensive—they charge a LOT—and then they pay a "wholesale" fee to a local attorney. Their priority is churning out cash rather than providing you with good counsel. Hiring someone from hundreds of miles away to handle your DUI is throwing your money away. When you can sit across the table from "your" lawyer, so that they can look you in the eye and find out the best way to help, you will feel better about your case and you gain the potential of getting the very best results. Knowing that the individual who is actually handling your case is only a phone call away, will make you feel more secure about the process and your outcome.

Cleaning Up Your Record

In California, the law provides a process to have convictions dismissed for the purpose of disclosure to an employer. The law recognizes that good jobs are hard to come by and that your employment prospects should not be scuttled forever just because you picked up a DUI conviction.

At the conclusion of your probation, you can have the case dismissed, pursuant to Penal Code section 1203.4. In order to be eligible, you must be off probation—this means for <u>any</u> offense. Second, you cannot have any pending criminal cases.

Once you have your case dismissed, you will not be required to disclose the conviction to an employer. However, you are required to disclose the conviction if you are applying for a professional license, such as credentials as a teacher, CPA, lawyer, doctor, etc. You also must disclose the conviction if you apply for a job with the lottery or law enforcement. Further, even with a dismissal, a DUI conviction will remain on your driving record and can be used as a prior conviction for ten years from the date of the offense. There is no legal mechanism to change this in California.

In most circumstances, if you are convicted of a DUI, you will be placed on probation for three years. In many counties, if you have paid off your fine, completed your "jail" time[21], completed your drinking driver school and any other conditions of probation, you can petition the court to terminate your probation early. Most counties have a policy that you must complete at least half of your probationary period. The court's willingness to do this is normally based upon the policy of the county. If there is an extraordinary justification, you can often get the court to grant this request. One example is if you are trying to enter the military. The military does not want to take people who are on active probation. If this was your first offense, and there is nothing complicating it, the court will often terminate probation early to allow you to serve.

You are entitled, as a matter of law, to have the case dismissed if you have probation terminated early or have completed the entire period. This process is not automatic; you must file a petition and, in most counties, pay a filing fee.[22] The court will have the probation department review your petition, determine if you have paid your fines, completed all of the conditions, and avoided any other violations. If you have been successful, you will have your petition granted. In some counties, the court will not require a court appearance.[23] In other

---

[21] This would include weekend work, work project, or other disciplinary period.
[22] Currently the statutory filing fee can be up to $150 (Penal Code section 1203.4(d)).
[23] Sacramento County, for example, does not require a court appearance, unless you are seeking to have probation terminated early.

counties, you or your lawyer will be required to show up to court to address this issue.

Even if you did not "successfully" complete probation, you can still have your case dismissed. A violation of probation can include committing a new crime, failure to pay your fines, failure to do your "jail" time, failure to do your drinking driver school or violation of any other condition the court imposed. In these circumstances, the court has the discretion to dismiss the case in the interest of justice. Obviously, you have some explaining to do. You will be required to explain to the court why you did not successfully complete probation and to provide a compelling reason why the court should grant you the relief you seek. This can be done at any time after probation has expired or terminated.

I often have clients come to my office with a prior conviction (DUI or otherwise) that is a decade or more old. They find that this is holding them back from getting employment and they want to do something about it. No matter how old the conviction, the court has the jurisdiction to dismiss the case. The court will generally grant these petitions, especially in the situation where you have not had a law violation for many years.

As a side note, if the conviction was a misdemeanor (as most DUI's are), you are not eligible for any further relief such as a Certificate of Rehabilitation or a governor's pardon.

Has Drinking Become a Problem in Your Life?

If you have been arrested and are facing jail time, a large fine, and a period of probation, this is a problem. To be sure, not everyone who is arrested for a DUI is an alcoholic or even has a "drinking problem."

If you are arrested for a DUI, I recommend you take a long and hard look at your drinking patterns and attitude. Unless you are one of the very rare people, this was not the first time that you drove under the influence of alcohol. You were just lucky in the past. Take time to take inventory and discuss your situation with the people who know you best. Ask for their honest assessment about what they think about your drinking habits. If alcohol or drugs have begun to take a toll on your life, maybe it is time to start to address the situation.

When clients come in to my office, I will have a frank and honest conversation with them about their drinking. I don't "get on my soap box", and I am certainly not a person who can sit in judgment of others. But, what I don't want are repeat DUI customers. I take the time to point out that they don't want to hurt or kill someone and have to live with that guilt. I take this seriously and feel a responsibility to be honest with my clients to try to avert any future problems. I want people to understand the danger they cause when they drive under the influence. Astonishingly, many times I am the first person to broach this subject.

I have had potential clients walk out the door when I start talking about their drinking issues. They simply don't want to hear it. They most likely are not yet ready to deal with this problem. However, I feel I owe it to my clients to be honest with my assessment regarding whether I believe that they have an issue that needs to be addressed. If I believe there is a drinking issue at hand, it is likely that the court and district attorney will see it the same way. I believe that affirmatively addressing the issue will pay benefits regarding sentencing and the final outcome -- and it may have life-changing results.

Whether it's AA, outpatient treatment, or inpatient treatment, many of my clients have literally saved their own lives by addressing an issue that was causing them a great deal of trouble.

Being Sued in Civil Court

If you are involved in an automobile accident while driving under the influence, there is a good chance that you will be sued in civil court for monetary damages. If this happens, the award for damages will be owed in addition to any restitution the criminal court granted.

In a civil suit, the victim can demand payment for "pain and suffering." This can be a very large amount and can be dependent, in large part, on what a jury feels a case is worth.

If sued in civil court, you can also be required to withstand depositions, interrogatories, and other discovery questions. Normally the criminal case will resolve long before the civil case even gets started. If the criminal matter is still pending when the civil case is filed, you can refuse to answer questions during a deposition or interrogatories.

If you have insurance, most likely your insurance company will provide you with an attorney and defend you in the civil suit. If you do not have insurance, you will have to either represent yourself or hire your own attorney.

Conclusion

Getting arrested for driving under the influence of alcohol, or drugs, is serious. It can be very complicated. Finding skilled and experienced counsel is critical to obtaining the best outcome possible and protecting your rights. I have given you some basic information in this book to help educate you so that you can make knowledgeable decisions.

Don't go it alone.

- Locate and retain a local attorney with a specific focus on DUI cases.
- Be honest with your lawyer and follow their advice.
- Have a good attitude and be respectful of the process and the court.
- If convicted, complete probation and have your case dismissed.

About the Author

Michael Chastaine, owner and founder of The Chastaine Law Office, has been practicing law for almost three decades. He spent the first half of his career as a Public Defender in Santa Clara County. He has handled thousands of DUI's, as well as all manner of serious felonies, including capital murder cases. He was the head of the Public Defender research department on several occasions, and has argued in front of the California Supreme Court.

Michael entered private practice in 2001 and opened his own firm – The Chastaine Law Office – in 2007. Since then, he has been selected to the *Best Lawyers in America* List, the *Northern California Super Lawyers* list and the *Top 100 DUI Attorneys* list by The National Advocacy for DUI Defense, for multiple years running.

When he is not advocating for his client's rights, Michael is a retired National Ski Patroller and is a competitive mountain bike racer and adventure racer.

Learn more at

www.YourSacDUIAttorney.com

or contact us at

support@chastainelaw.net

How to Survive a DUI Arrest:

What You NEED to Know

Call our office TODAY
(916) 932-7150

Mention this book and receive a
FREE CONSULTATION
<u>(A $300 value)</u>

Let us help you get the VERY best results after your DUI arrest

www.YourSacDUIAttorney.com

DON'T GO IT ALONE!

Made in the USA
San Bernardino, CA
30 September 2017